Nature Upclose

A House Spider's Life

Written and Illustrated by John Himmelman

Children's Press®
A Division of Grolier Publishing
New York London Hong Kong Sydney
Danbury, Connecticut

For "Five Legs," the house spider that lived above my desk while I worked on this book

Library of Congress Cataloging-in-Publication Data

Himmelman, John
    A house spider's life / written and illustrated by John Himmelman.
        p.   cm. — (Nature upclose)
    Includes biographical references.
    ISBN 0-516-21185-4 (lib.bdg.) 0-516-26536-9(pbk.)
    1. Achaearanea tepidariorum—Juvenile literature.
I. Series: Himmelman, John. Nature upclose.
QL458.42.T54H56   1999
595.4'4—dc21   98-52384
                                                        CIP
                                                        AC

House Spider
Achaearanea tepidariorum

House spiders are found throughout North America. They belong to a group of spiders called "cobweb weavers." They are responsible for most of the webs that suddenly appear in our homes.

A house spider is most active at night. That is the best time to watch it working on its web. Although a house spider rests during the day, it will take action the moment an insect lands on its web. The spider approaches the insect from beneath the web, wraps it in silk, injects it with venom, and feeds on it through a pair of fanglike structures called chelicerae (kuh-LIHS-uh-ree).

It is not unusual for many generations of house spiders to live in the same house. House spiders usually live a little more than a year from the time they become adults. Some males live shorter lives because females may eat them after the spiders mate.

A young house spider crawls out of an *egg sac*.

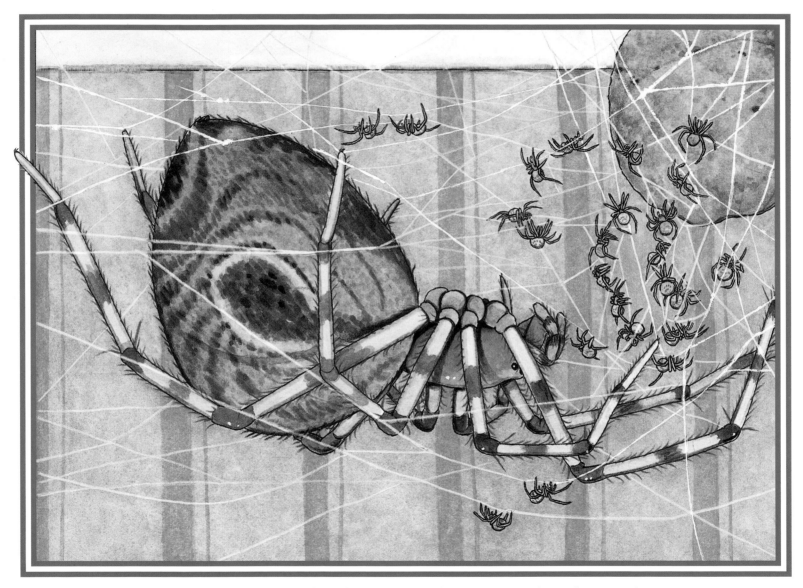

She joins the other *spiderlings* in her mother's web.

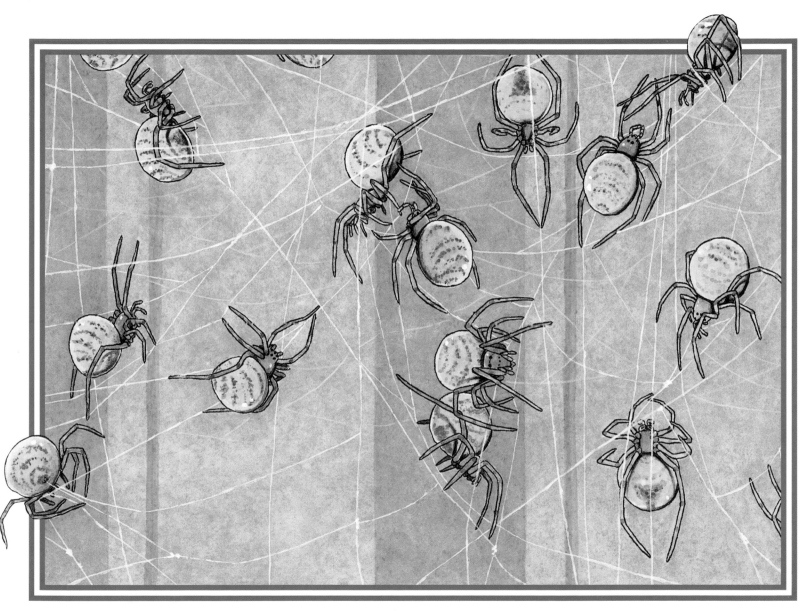

The spiderlings stay together for several weeks.

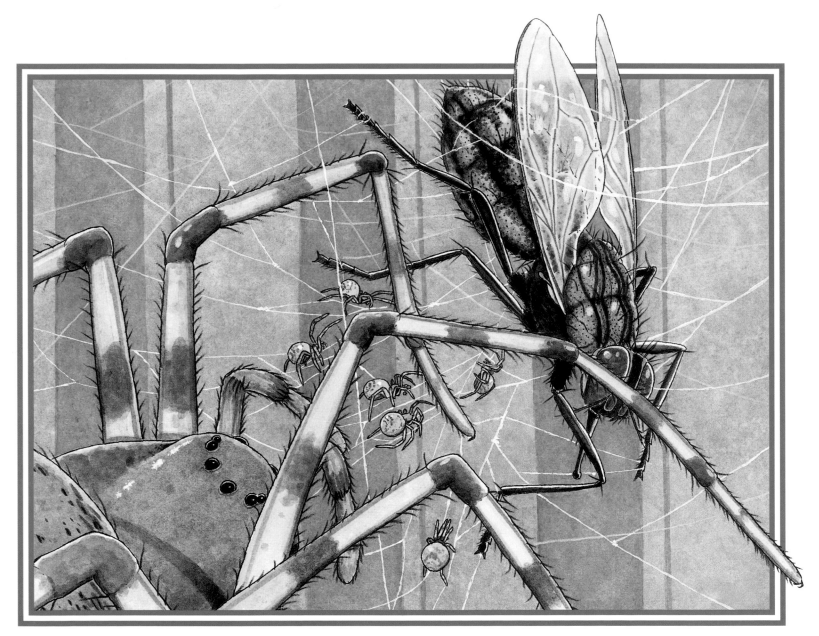

A *house fly* lands on the web.

It breaks free. The spiderling is carried away.

She lands on a bookshelf . . .

. . . and weaves her own little web of *silk.*

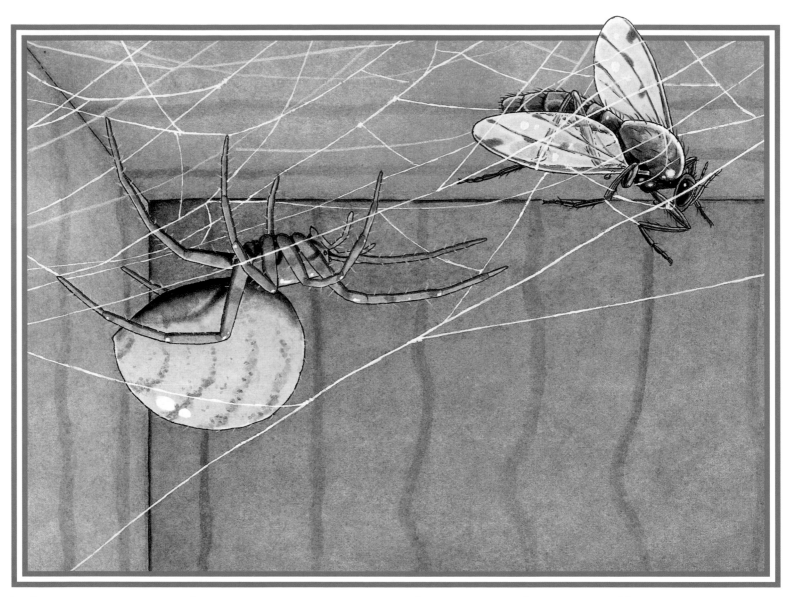

The young spider is strong enough to catch a small insect.

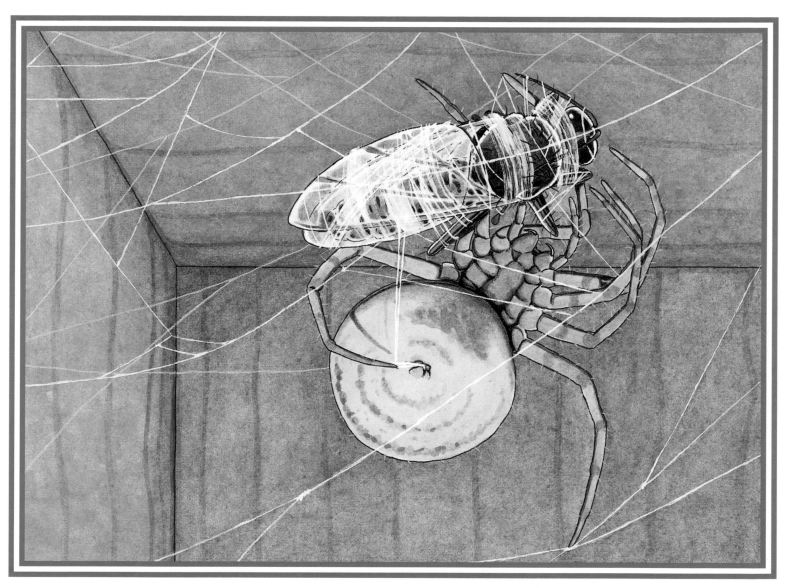

She wraps it in silk so it can't get away.

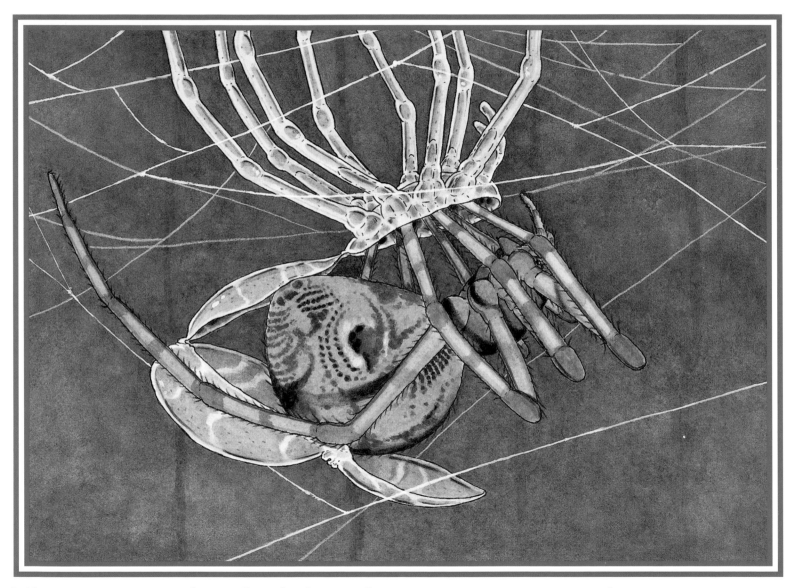

The young spider sheds her skin many times as she grows.

Soon she is a full-grown spider.

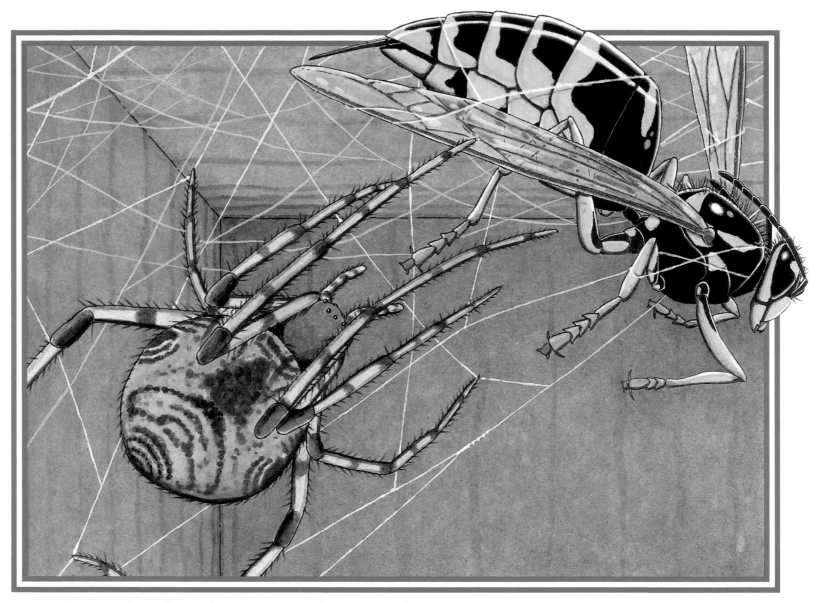

A *yellow jacket* flies into her web.

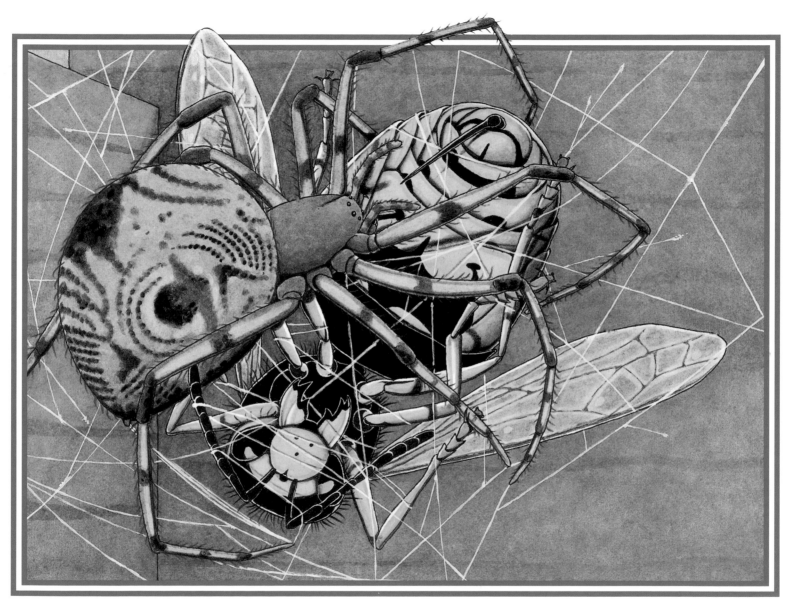

They fight a dangerous battle.

The house spider wins. Now she has enough food for a week.

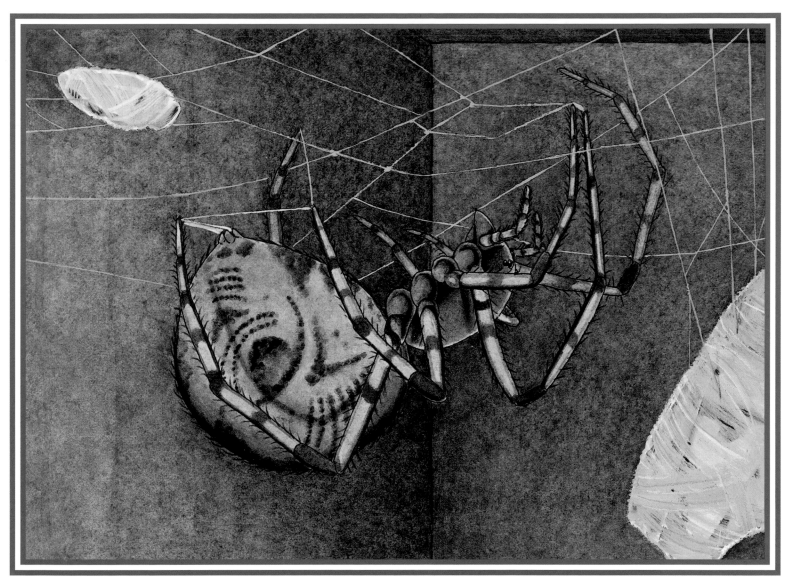

The spider spends the evening fixing her web.

In the morning, a vacuum cleaner sucks it away!

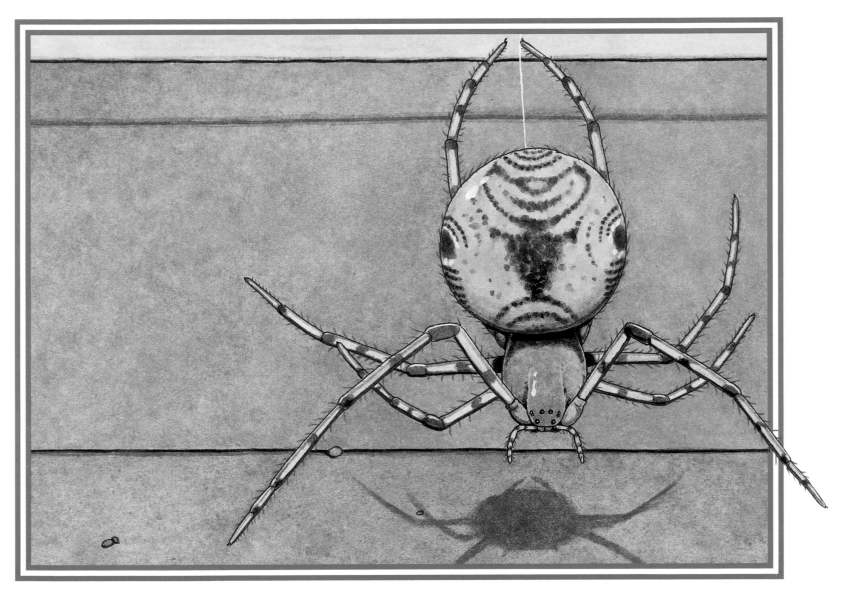

The house spider escapes by dropping to the floor.

She climbs up the stairs . . .

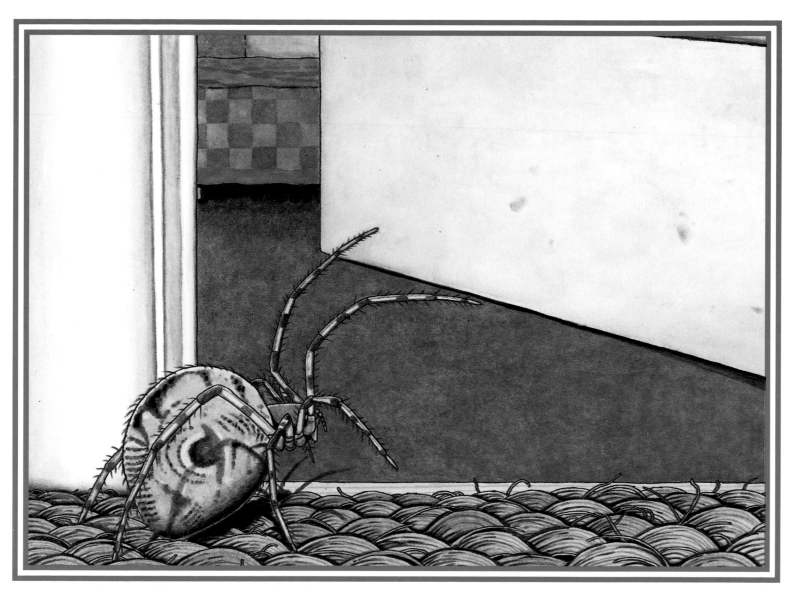

. . . and walks into a bedroom.

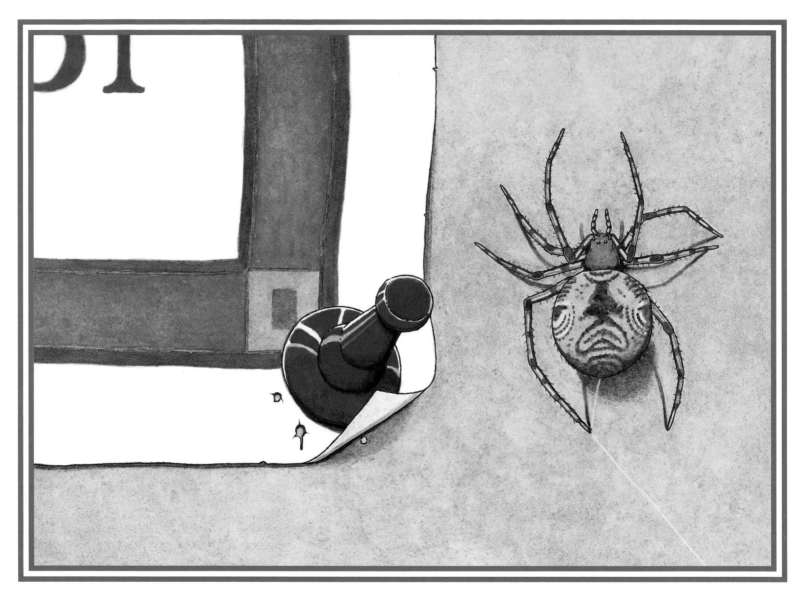

She crawls up a wall . . .

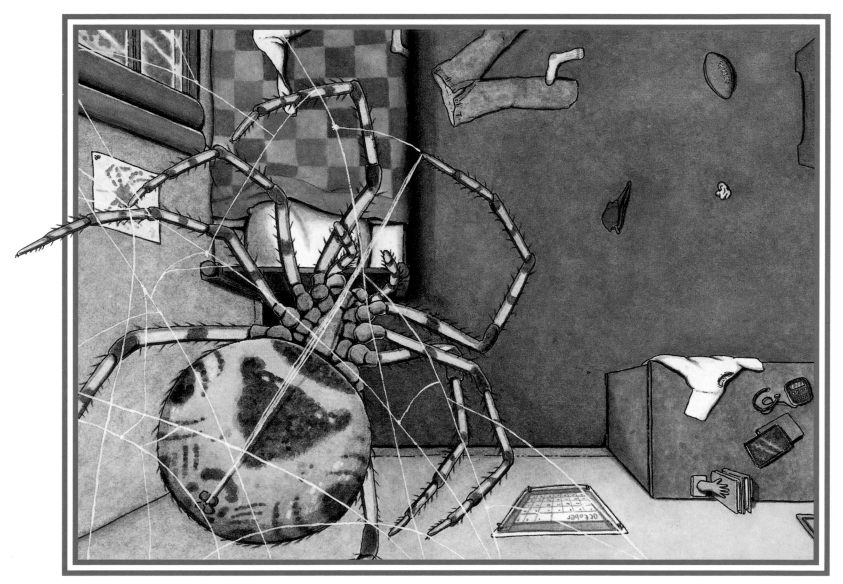

. . . and finds the perfect spot for a new web.

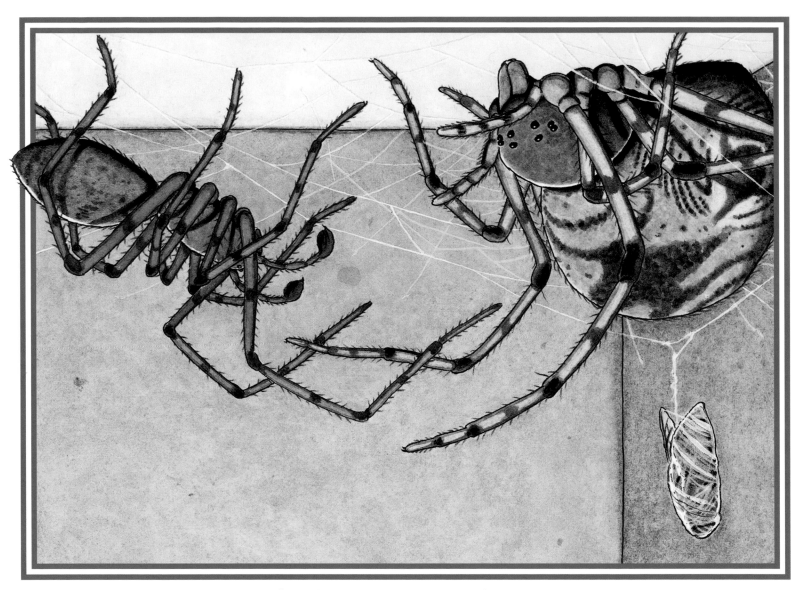

A male house spider finds her new web.

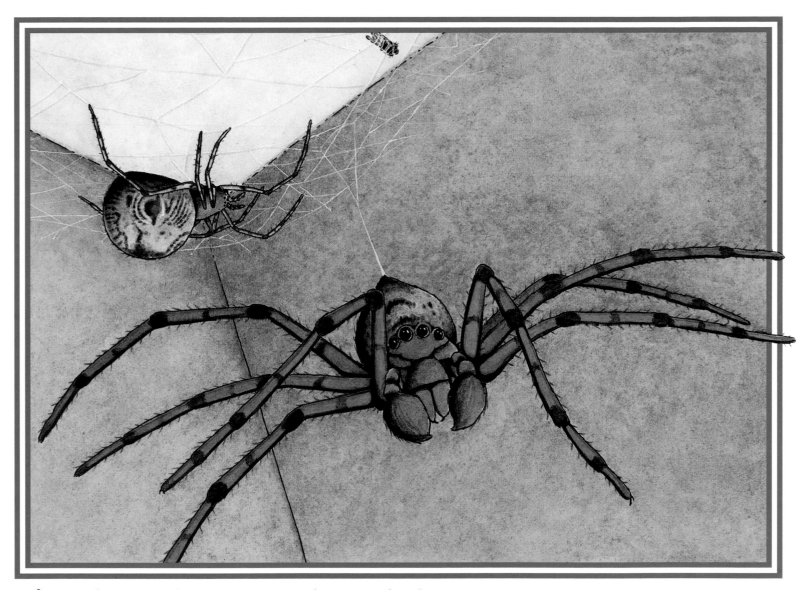

After the spiders mate, the male leaves.

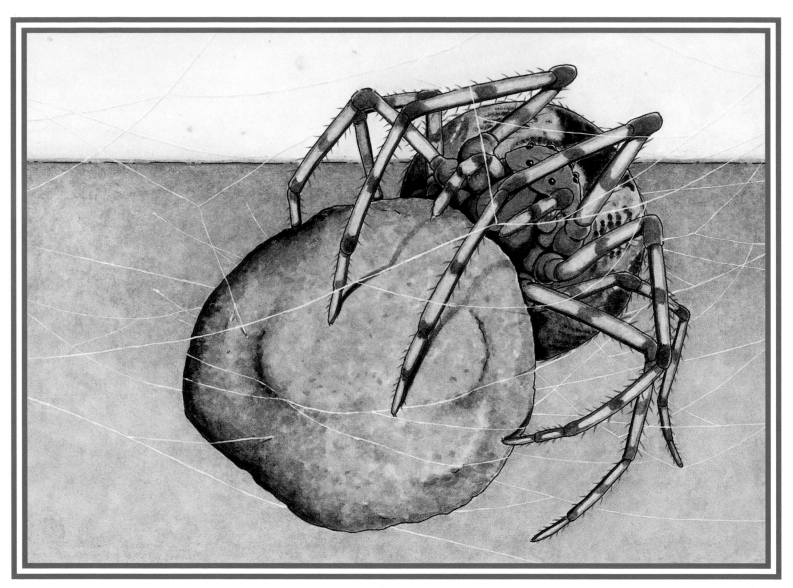

Soon the house spider lays eggs. She wraps them in a silk
egg sac.

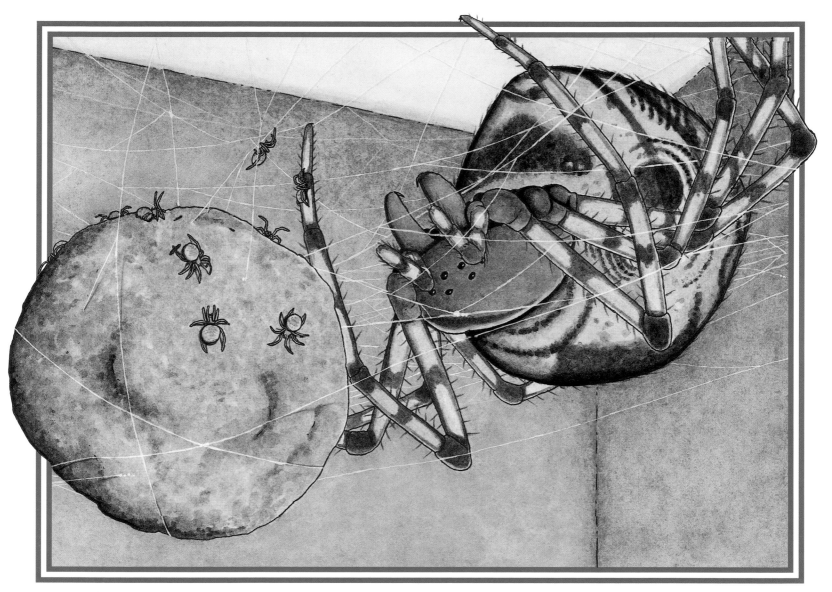

In a few weeks, her spiderlings crawl out.

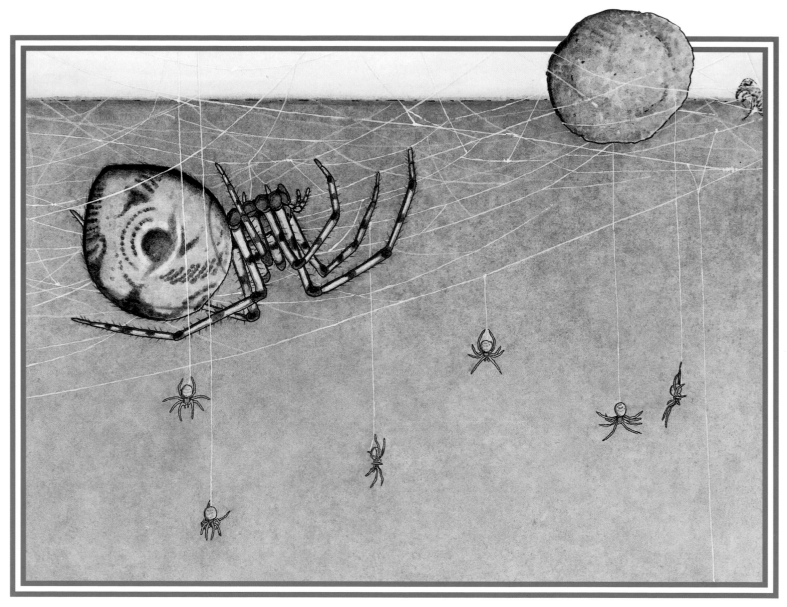

Eventually, the spiderlings leave their mother's web.

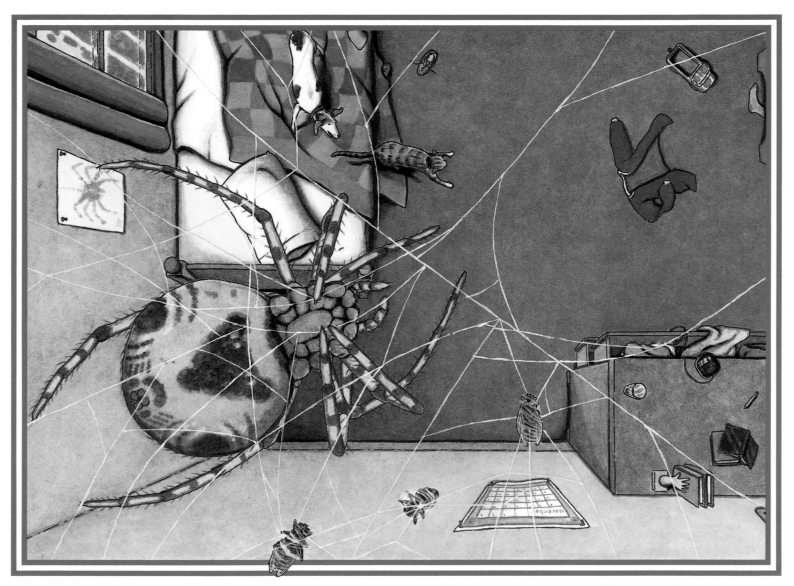

But the bedroom will be her home for the rest of her days . . .

. . . and the rest of her nights.

Words You Know

egg sac—a group of eggs wrapped in silk. The silk keeps the eggs safe.

house fly—a flying insect commonly found in homes.

silk—a threadlike material that spiders use to move from place to place, build webs, wrap their eggs, and catch insects.

spiderling—the first stage of a spider's life.

yellow jacket—a stinging insect that is closely related to bees and wasps.

About the Author

John Himmelman has written or illustrated more than forty books for children, including *Ibis: A True Whale Story*, *Wanted: Perfect Parents*, *J.J. Versus the Babysitter*, and eight other books in the Nature Upclose series. His books have received honors such as Pick of the List, Book of the Month, JLG Selection, and the ABC Award. He is also a naturalist who enjoys turning over dead logs, crawling through grass, kneeling over puddles, and gazing at the sky. His greatest joy is sharing these experiences with others. John lives in Killingworth, Connecticut, with his wife, Betsy, who is an art teacher. They have two children, Jeff and Liz.